Adam Horovitz

Love and Other Fairy Tales

Indigo Dreams Publishing

First Edition: Love and Other Fairy Tales
First published in Great Britain in 2021 by:
Indigo Dreams Publishing Ltd
24 Forest Houses
Halwill
Beaworthy
EX21 5UU
www.indigodreams.co.uk

ISBN 978-1-912876-65-5

British Library Cataloguing in Publication Data. A CIP record for this book can be obtained from the British Library.

Designed and typeset in Palatino Linotype by Indigo Dreams.
Cover image, 'A Voice in the Woods' by © Tom Brown.
www. hopelessmaine.com

Printed and bound in Great Britain by 4edge Ltd.

Papers used by Indigo Dreams are recyclable products made from wood grown in sustainable forests following the guidance of the Forest Stewardship Council.

To the memory of my father, Michael Horovitz (1935 - 2021)
and of my friend Rick Vick (1948 - 2019)
who, between them, knew many of my ways through these
woods.

Acknowledgements

Many of these poems have appeared in magazines or online: thanks are due to Acumen, Ambit, Bakings, Bare Fiction, Horizon, Interlitq, New Departures, Outposted, Tears in the Fence, Verse Kraken and Versopolis.

Others have appeared in the following anthologies: *1914: Poetry Remembers* (Faber), *Christmas Poems vol. 7* (Candlestick), *Dear World* (Frosted Fire), *Grandchildren of Albion* (New Departures), *A Hatchery of Shadows* (SciPo), *Hwaet* (Bloodaxe), *The Orange Dove of Fiji* (Hutchinson), *The Physic Garden* (Palewell), *A Poem for Europe* (competition anthology), *The Poetry of Sex* (Penguin), *Stroud Poets anthology vol. 1* (Yew Tree) and the 2012 Wenlock Poetry Festival anthology.

'February in the Physic Garden' was written as a commission during my tenure as Herefordshire poet in residence.

Just over a third of this manuscript was written on a Hawthornden Fellowship.

I am very grateful to Katy Evans-Bush for casting her sharp editorial eye over this manuscript.

Also by Adam Horovitz:

Turning (Headland, 2011)
A Thousand Laurie Lees (The History Press, 2014)
Only the Flame Remains (Yew Tree, 2014)
The Physic Garden (ed.) (Palewell, 2017)
The Soil Never Sleeps (Palewell, 2018)
The Soil Never Sleeps (*2nd extended edition*) (Palewell, 2019)

CONTENTS

Conditions of Living

Commemoration Hour 11

Inner City Duende 14

I Used to Walk Through London 15

Returning to Frankfurt 16

The Singing Street 18

Orcop Christmas 20

Written on Shrove Tuesday, thinking of Seder 21

Fire-voices 22

The Afterlife of Dietrich Bonhoeffer 24

Conditions of Living 26

The Big Elevate Themselves 27

The Long Earth 28

February in the Physic Garden 29

The Eye of the God 31

Stopping with a bicycle on a hill above Stroud 34

Love and Other Fairy Tales

A Rose By Any Other Shape 39

There's a Music 40

At the Isolation Disco 41

Experiment 42

Murmuration 43

42nd Dream of You 44

To be Read Looking Upward Over Water 45

Lost to the Body 46

Seed and Stone 47

Like Rain 48

At the End 49

Tears Like Lava 50

The Reflection Answers Narcissus 51

Off the Map...52

Holiday in Arden...53

Love Poem Disguised as a Fairy Tale.................................55

Last Thoughts of the Unicorn...56

Fragment of a Fairy Tale Caught in a Time Loop...............58

Thisbë the Verse 59

Some Kind of Fairy Tale...60

Beyond the Gates 61

Love Like Pollen...62

The Marriage of Consonant and Vowel..............................63

Coda..65

Love and Other Fairy Tales

Conditions of Living

Commemoration Hour

A moth-cupped flame
sputters out of silence in my kitchen, draws
insects whining through the window's crack.

They sing like distant bi-planes,
dogfight-dancing at the edge of sight.

I watch red wax spill
over the candle's battered lip,
think of family, long dead,

the quiet men on unquiet fronts
who let the rituals of their religion

slide away, buoyed up
on propaganda, desperation, hunger,
as they wrote loving letters in the dark

succoured only by a single flame,
by the guttering distances of home.

Oh, how they dreamed of family,
gave thanks to G-d for the minuscule mercies
of the weekly post (when it got through)

but even the gentlest men will break inside
when bombs and snipers dictate their diet,

when all the animals of hell
come crawling out from under mud
on sinews of metal clasping at the bone.

*

What precisely did they die for,
or limp home wounded with?

My grandfather never said, sitting in silence
with his memories in the garden of his weekend home
until he was forced to cross Germany's borders
and escape into England two decades on.

Great Uncle Martin could not say,
splintered in 1915 by enemy fire. Only his letters remain
regaling his dearest sister Röschen
with brotherly bravado; detailing requests
for the essentials: paper, food and pens;
whatever news might make it through the lines from home.

*

This candle's spitting out its last
one hundred years on
but still the news is limited and grim.

The insect whine of war continues.
Tanks rumble through my kitchen
whenever the fridge fires up.

Commemoration wears an ugly, celebratory mask.
Its eyeholes stare us down like guns
and from its mouth a fine gas seeps.

'Gas! Quick, boys.' An ecstasy of fumbling
in the press for ways to not quite say
We won, we won, we won!

But we won nothing. The war continues
in fragments, though no one is yet
crazed enough to join the dots,

and all I can see in this quiet hour
is red wax stiffening on the candle
into the faces of all the people that I love.

Inner City Duende

Now she is clockwork in the bus lanes,
a bottled-up tock of sorrow.
All her straight lines are strung
through a maze of stuttering street lamps.

A slow build in the beer barrels
to this, the banshee hour
    louder than trains
the rhythms of her misery

running on iron rods down
into the hot bright
hells of Angel, Euston,
Camden Town.

The city swallows her,
binds her in tarmac,
trails pleasures behind her;
a constellation of fractured glass.

She weeps mascara.
Her eyes are ideograms, untranslatable,
as she slashes the brambling
arms of friends away.

And then she is dancing
to the dark sounds of her sorrow,
the city's breath rising through her
as she ripples, divided, multiplied,

like a water-bound moon slipping
through shop windows,
as street neon carves her tears
into the lights of cars.

I Used to Walk Through London

and always the edge lands
drew my eye, the sharp borders
between estates where decay
and order met – the wildernesses
where willowherb and ivy
argued for space amongst bricks.

The city's hum drowned
by insects – broken hieroglyphs
of graffitied wall matched colour
for colour by a riot of small flowers
and butterflies that shuddered
through nettles like ghosts of progress.

These were my brief gardens,
deep in the soft places where nature
reimagined itself, pushed up
against the weight of human rot
and choked at its histories
until they fell to sediment and dust.

Like a prophecy of our absence
these places let through piece by piece
a chronicle of suspended seed,
millennia old, from beneath the tarmac.
I used to walk through London, watch
plant life learning how to out-dream us.

Returning to Frankfurt

Mid-morning's landlocked heat
claws over new stone dressed to look ancient.
Rises above banks and museums
palpable as steam until the city

shivers into a state of imbalance.
A tipping point between this exact
moment of perception and all those
yesterdays we came here to discover.

My father moves through a clenched
box of sunlight caught between trees
radiant in his sweat-dishevelled suit.
His smile is child-like, a little lost

in the streets of a home he can't remember,
has extrapolated from anecdote, song,
discussion as it was mourned over decades;
locked into the long passages of childhood,

wound tight as myth. The city's a deep
bruise of longing, its foundations persistent
almost as the ceremonies, sacraments and family
tunes carried across Europe, over centuries.

Hineni. Here we are. Eighty years since he left
nestled in his mother's arms aged two
and though we walk past cemetery walls
scarred with familiar names, grief slips away

in the heat-baffled grandeur of a city remade
to celebrate that which was lost amongst
all that has been regained, renewed. He sings
as the river Main sings, a soft breath under bridges,

round street corners, past Turkish falafel stalls.
Ancestor tunes guide us through city sweat
to the museum where their memories reside.
And the city bids us welcome, welcome.

The Singing Street
a Sunderland memory

Coming home from school early,
we step to the soft rattle of kets in paper,
galaxies of sugar stretched across our lips.
I whistle with a stolen valve cap stuffed
between my fingers, wait for Phil's shrilled reply.
We manoeuvre through enemy territory,
the deeper yells of Thornhill teenagers
propelling us homewards.

We are planning our escapes for later;
along the chattering teeth of broken walls,
into the big garden two streets down
where no one ever finds us in our maze
of birdsong and leaf crunch; or shrieking like seagulls
by Mowbray Park on creaking bicycles, flashing
through streets where music and television
merge into a song of hunger.

But first, home and supper.
The door clicks and I am back inside,
in the still house where students rustle
like gentle ghosts upstairs
and, in the converted pantry, my mother sighs in the bath
                – but not tonight. Tonight
there is a small cry from the bedroom,
a cub cry, a whimpering.

I knock and call: *Is everything alright?*
The cry intensifies, becomes musical,
a two part harmony, a dance of tongues.
No one is answering me.

I knock again.
Are you in pain? I ask, and *Can I help?*
The duet becomes opera and I retreat,
hot faced and frightened, to the singing street.

Kets — Sweets

Orcop Christmas

That final Christmas, I hunted for Orcop's holy thorn
along lanes narrowed by bronze-black leaves,
peered through hedgerows starved of birdsong
into winter-dithered pasture, sought the miraculous
promissory wink of white December stars.

I found no field-feast of light, no hawthorn
where I'd read it stood; just cigarettes in the verge –
nine rattling in a twenty box. I climbed a tree,
belched gouts of votive smoke across the lane
and, for the last time willingly, I prayed.

Back home, my mother said *A Christmas quest!*
and laughed although it hurt. She held my cheek.
You're not quite Galahad, more Gawain with that hair.
The thorn died in a storm two years ago. I'm sure I said...
Tear-clenched, I withdrew

until fire lit the kitchen for a feast. We sat to eat,
firm rods of lurcher chin pressed to our laps,
witness to the one small miracle the day allowed:
my mother, briefly strong again amongst
the hedgerow hallows that wreathed the room

a passing grace that hid in smoke
the way the cancer kept shaving her to light.

Written on Shrove Tuesday, thinking of Seder

All my beliefs are swallowed or unsaid.
Bitter herbs and fruits sting my throat like guilt.
Where does the mouth lead? Belly, heart or head?

My mother's pancakes. Sugar lemon spread.
A shriving, a taunt on memory's tongue.
All my beliefs are swallowed or unsaid.

The Seder sandwich. Horseradish, flat bread;
an apple sauce, smooth and sweeter than truth.
Where does the mouth lead? Belly, heart or head?

One pinch of sweetness and one pinch of dread.
Salt songs of sorrow ground down to a meal.
All my beliefs are swallowed or unsaid.

Hope is a hunger, a sliver, a shred,
a tear in the cloth, a focus for fear.
Where does the mouth lead? Belly, heart or head?

The pancake's flipped out, the matzoh's a thread
and I have nothing to put in their place.
All my beliefs are swallowed or unsaid.
Where does the mouth lead? Belly, heart or head?

Fire-voices

What is religion?
A shared dream of landscape
fenced with simple rules

by which to live a life of listening
for the quivering fire-voice of hope;
       some spark of kindness
in the desert's inward creep.

    *

Does it still the hand
that wields a knife? No,
not always, but it is built to do so;

at least until some chancer learns
how easy it can be to throw
their voice into the fire.
Thereafter, watch the fences burn
and as they burn, watch
how the gentler truths they held mutate
into a cancer-rush of fright;

how people begin listening
to any siren song that panders to their fears,
in a flame that someone else has set.
New fences (ten feet tall and charged
with panic by the lightning bolt) will soon spring up
and then there's nothing left except
to be livestock in someone else's bonfire,

screamed at till you cannot wake,
until all that's left of thought
is the desire to fight.

    *

What is faith? The tending
of empty places where structures
fail to find a foothold.

The act of reaching out
for a quivering fire-voice of hope;
        some spark of kindness
in the desert's inward creep.

The Afterlife of Dietrich Bonhoeffer

i *Bonhoeffer imprisoned*

Nothing to do but smoke and study
the emptiness of time, wait with my books
for the guards to arrive,
swearing like knives, stamping out the cold.

Cruelty settles only on my skin, like ink
until the pen's bled dry. Who
is Christ for us today?
A sharpening of tools in the antechamber.

The mansion of their father has many
rooms lined with metal teeth.
We learned too late; it is not the thought
but readiness to take responsibility.

What use the edifice, the structure, if
in building it we throttle and dismember?

ii *A survivor remembers the road to extinction*

A long road in April
under American mortar
but he was calm, so calm,
as if prison
had eaten nothing of him.

The guards wept sweat and blood,
jittered like kittens
on the approach to Flossenbürg.
If they were praying, no one heard but Bonhoeffer
or, if there's such a creature, God.

Asked for a Sunday service
before the rope, he read Isiah in the mud.
With his wounds we are healed.
So many wounded gods out there.
Which one to choose?

Conditions of Living

Once, we died dreaming and drowning
in the first flush of youth,
our bones yellowing beneath our skins.
We died standing up,
propped on our spears,

watching the world subsume us
in a winding cloth of sand.
We fell with our cattle and our crops
when winter swallowed us
like nightmares in a dream of sun.

Now, we are always in the light
but still we're fearful.
The world spins faster. We see the atoms dancing
in our minds and slow our ageing,
hide behind our mobile phones

check our profiles
in the darkened mirrors of the web.
We cannot recognise ourselves.
Instinct is caged in ancient bodies
which in their turn are caged in metal.

The land grows meat instead of trees
and all the world's a stage that hates its players
who strut and forget
that they are only
        scuffed knuckles on a fist of rock.

The Big Elevate Themselves

"Every crowd has a silver lining." ~ Phineas Taylor Barnum

Barnum's elephant ambles into Minnesota skies
in a silver, quilted jacket of hydrogen;
a trumpeting blimp
for the greatest show on earth.
He is blissful, dances with the clouds,
which scatter, jealous of his metallic sheen.

Free from the plough
they used to hitch on him to draw the punters in
he back-flips, bounces, swivels like the clowns,
does not look down
to see the awe-struck crowd he's drawn
offering up their silver lining.

Barnum's elephant is content
to call this his own achievement.
He does not want to see the puffed up
smile on Barnum's face.
The big may elevate themselves, he thinks.
At least I've done it with some grace.

The Long Earth
after the books by Terry Pratchett and Stephen Baxter

If all it took was just a sideways step
to break your shackle to this tired earth,
untangle the strings of quantum physics
and shimmer down the mirror parallel,
find worlds which Darwin could have barely dreamed,
would you not do it? Would you not run?

I'd be off faster than the starting gun
to seek the Long Earth flickering un-reamed;
new genera and what mutations dwell
under different suns. I'd hunt strange musics
courting river banks, mountains and the surf.
If all it took were but a sideways step.

Yet here we stay. There is no interstitial strait,
just dreams. The faith of science. All that we create.

February in the Physic Garden
At Hellens, Much Marcle, Herefordshire

The garden's still.
Budless. A monochrome sky
has locked it out of spring.

Last year's ghost-stalk crop
stands guard,
holds the soil to account,

shivers in the breeze
as worms and insects
knead the earth around its roots.

> *Knitbone. Garlic. Yarrow for a jagged wound.*
> *All the plants for poultice and binding placed*
> *side by side, carefully, in bed with Betony*
> *and Chamomile; dream-safe, digestion's aid.*

Eight sections to the garden,
following the phases of the moon.
A millennia's root-weave of learning,

the raised bed of Ceridwen's cauldron
open to centuries of trial and error.
Three drops of wisdom for every tongue

from the octagonal seed-hoard,
divided and quarter-mastered,
waiting for the coming sun.

> *Spells for the sorcerer, lost in the Earth's shadow.*
> *Wolfsbane, Wormwood, Lily of the Valley.*
> *The swift flight of the Henbane oracle,*
> *its yellow head lifting you on dragon-wing leaves.*

Not long now until the Earth's turning
winds time up to its swiftest tick
and Skullcap's tiny calyx dish

pushes out towards the light,
amongst the slow creep of Heartsease,
the lingering Christmas Rose.

Light is a medicine for medicine,
a poultice to soothe the garden's
hardy, winter-prickled skin.

The Eye of the God
after listening to Holst's Jupiter

sat at the edge of a wood,
the point where it spills
open onto the lip of a hill,
        the valley
snaps into focus
as street lights
        spit into life

                a map
        of undiscovered stars

I look away from the dark
mirror of the town, up
        past this orange fist
of man-made safety measures
towards the eye
        of the god

        *

        it is time
to travel outwards
                forget
                that I am
                sitting still
into the vacuum,
        the great
        expanse, the place
                of nothingness and multitudes

    seek the only
        breath that matters,
    the oxygen of joy

*

may it burn in my blood
          like the storms
          of Jupiter

**

There's another country, a place
where pleasure is bundled and bound
to the duty of sunlight. Yes, the people
equivocate there, talk up the motions of space
in all earnestness as if the planets are sheep
that move like clouds, in brownian sympathy,
laced across a high hillside, stark as a dead planet.
In this country, the atmosphere's erased.
Last shreds of happiness are steepled
into too-high-towers that will not last the hour
                    of their building.

This is not my country, this place where small
pleasures are the only substitute for joy.
No grace there, only a powdered poverty.
No vow that lasts more than a week
                    in the structured, suffocating void.

**

take me back to pre-electric nights
          a time when arenas of hope were written
in albino freckles across the patterned
          mouth of space

it need only be
for a moment

I will follow the white bull down moonlit, sacred paths
to the place of sacrifice where sour realities
alchemise into joy – listen for the blood-call
    'to Jove, best and greatest'

        as his febrile eye blinks out
        ecstatic drops of light

Stopping with a bicycle on a hill above Stroud thinking of Ivor Gurney

Five valleys splay below me
like a broken hand encased in mud.
From this high point, I see
open veins of streams running
in rivulets toward the Severn's
metallic, distant slice of light and water.

I stand beside a hedgerow
that's been growing cancerous for years
from the broken wall my bike
is parked against. It was shrub
and bramble when I cycled past it
lazy on my way to school.

It rages, now, like a negative of fire
held still against the winter sky,
and I think of Gurney casting back
from Flanders with his pen
at a different angle, to take the same
landscape in, as if it were breath.

      *

The road is quiet. No traffic
on the way from Bisley. Only buzzards
and the ghosts of babies
whose un-christened road-deaths, centuries back,
formed the town below. A new form,
the 'perfections / of flowers and petal and blade'.

But landscapes shift. Wild spaces
are surrounded and look starker for it,
stranger, briefly, until litter intercedes.
Mankind's interactions wane and wax;
old walls collapse, new ones
clatter up the sky like angry pigeons.

*

A sheep in the field turns to bleat at me,
as if surprised by the tyrannies of change.
What would we recognise,
Gurney and I? The Severn's progress,
like a scarred, unbroken sword
shot through with filigrees of winter light.

The aching yell of gulls
flown eastward after ploughs. The way
the sun sinks like a cuticle
into a skin of cloud. The foreboding sense,
something new we can't be part of.
What rides this dusk like a pheromone.

The bicycle calls me to the hill, the wind,
the last hawk-dive into Friday night. No more
listening to spectres; no more pauses
on cold hills to mourn the sun.
'…the earth that ploughs
forgets protestation in its turning…'

Love and Other Fairy Tales

A Rose By Any Other Shape

That old anarchist Love
insists that a rose by any other shape
is still a rose,
that split atoms remember the world
before the changes came
                in mushroom-throes.

That old anarchist Love
demands that rain forget
that it was ever clouds or sea
and will continue to be so
on and off
                perpetually.

That old anarchist Love
is out again and breaking hearts –
rekindling old desires with a thorny sting
then, with surgeon's aim,
beating down the bones of winter
                to make way for spring.

That old anarchist Love
rides the air like honeysuckle musk.
Upsets apple carts, tips over Eden's tables.
Moulds passion from the clays of hope.
Chases dust from sorrow. Turns friendships
                into fables.

        That old anarchist Love
        descends like a fist of summer rain.
        That old anarchist Love
        teaches the world to fall in lust again.

There's a Music

Listen. There's a music in your head
that is not some half-remembered bar
of radio confection. No ear-worm, this.
No broadcast soaked up by the soft
core of childhood. It sits among synapses
as a code of scars, a Morse-mapped monument.
This music is made from the friction of living:
birdsong; the passage of light at a certain
time of day; the first touch of another's skin;
that moment when everything seemed exact.
Built upon pain and plenty, this concentrated
sound is everything you know and understand
tuned up to ecstasy. Written and unwritten
in the key of hope. Yet it is not complete.
Now, having listened, you must sing a tender
approximation of the tune (as sweetly as you can)
until all the people who have helped it build
are drawn to you. And then you must dance.

At the Isolation Disco

the past wobbles from speakers,
fills your hastily cleared room
with the noise and sweat of memory.

> Conjure the image of a lover
> in the haze-space between beats.
> Imagine their dance as you shiver

with want. Move to them. Move away.
Return smiling. You could almost
be sharing drinks and kisses

> here in the proximity of longing,
> spiked with a micro-dose of hope
> as the furniture fades to nothing

and the beat drops harder, until at last
the isolation disco presses back
against the hollow ache of silence

> in euphoric whooshes. Fills lungs
> with a hunger, a pressed lust,
> an anthem to carry you beyond solitude

into the shock of someone else's arms.

Experiment

Here is my hand. If I reach out
and let the nerves beneath my fingers' skin
shiver in sympathy with yours
I believe that my head will electrify itself,
split apart the atom of my lips,
create a fiery, autonomic smile.

The fine forest on my arms
will dance an implacable storm-dance,
tender and enraged.
Every cell of me will sing
in double helix harmony.
Only my eyes will remain intent and still.

Here is my hand. Will you take it? I'd like
to know if we can multiply this thrill.

Murmuration

We have taken the wrong path.
Our breath cottons on to bare November scrub
as we race thin sunlight up over bramble,
seeking the viewpoint where town and fields
stretch out below us, reaching
each for other in tender desperation.

At last we find the arrow-line to the hilltop
where you have promised starlings
clustered in clouds, landscape dazed by the clatter
of ten thousand pairs of wings, light stretched
into a constellation of feathers
beating in time to winter's breath.

We aim for the furthest mottled bench.
Other people have gathered. They took
easier routes, are insignificant as flies
and slide away like wind-blown newsprint
as starlings gather in ecstatic ones and twos
then bubble into hieroglyphic throngs.

So many paths I think, amazed,
as they sweep the fractured day
into coppered strata, wound incandescent
along the hidden track-line of the sea.
Such silences. And under them, the murmur
of cloth as you lift your face to the sky, throat

sheer as a path up to a mountain spring.
The birds settle into reed-bed roosts.
Their slow-stilled song sifts up through the ring
of trees around the hill. Our speech becomes sudden,
surreptitious, breathy. Something has shifted.
Conversation circles in a sky where paths are never wrong

and starlings dance the cautious path to bed.

42nd Dream of You

This time, you lead me
along a rain-bruised lane
ripe with the aniseed scent
of crushed cow parsley.

An ever-unreachable yard ahead,
your smile is bound tight as ivy
as you dance past blood spots
of campion, beckoning,

calling, laughing; your voice seductive
as the slow chant of tree branches
that bend to an imagined breeze.
Come, you whisper. I keep on coming,

incautious, stumble on loose stones,
on the invisible track the badgers make
nightly across tarmac, as they snarl
territorial love songs to the cloud-locked moon.

Through a shifting map of hedgerows
I watch you become birdsong, a smile
of light at the open window,
an invitation to enter into day.

To be Read Looking Upward Over Water

Travelled home with the taste of you
soft in my mouth. Spent the journey laughing
easy as stream water over last scraps of ice

breath crazed on the carriage window
        its patterns condensing
into a ghosted close-up of your face

while the vulgar winter sun
crooned hangover songs from the sea's stomach.
I pressed deeper in. The train's glass membrane

        planted a cool kiss on my illuminated eyelids

as sky blurred, slid sideways, became
fathomable (again, at last), the clouds
pulsing from grey to silver, outwards

into a white semaphore, a new lexicon
born from the breaking of long winter silences
to be read looking upward over water

punctuated by black dots
of wading birds, wide expanses of sand
and mudflats that are as skin

        ecstatic under the tongue of the tide.

Lost to the Body

A tide curls through us,
salts our tongues with words,
the urgency of their unknotting.

There's a pornographic opera
nightingales sing
locked in the wine cupboard.

The hushed laughter of women
gives us the library. The river is ours
their absence tells us,

its water delicate
as gorse flowers. The farmyard's
silvering. Trees in shock of leaf.

A week lost to the body,
seed moon a hobby lantern
guiding us seaward

as we sow new names for spring.

Seed and Stone

And sometimes we wake tangled up like reeds
in the ploughed, watered hollows of the bed,
the room alive with thought-drift; orchid seeds
dust-dancing through the sun's cold morning thread.

Or we rise swiftly, burrs hooked in our hair,
carry last night's barbs out into the light
to drop on the forgetful soil. Somewhere
they'll grow tall. Seed someone else's slight.

If time allows, we'll wrap our dreams in flesh,
hang on the branch of the bed as we swell
into each other: a seed-scape, a mesh.
A clot of longing in a pithy shell.

There are so many stems to push from seed and stone.
We are not built to lie dormant, too long alone.

Like Rain

A last sight of you
through the reflected
sea of a grubby railway window

on a bench below the bus stop,
facing me, framed in cloud.
I raise my hand. You hunch

into your raincoat, do not look up.
The carriage lurches, beats
faster at my ribs.

You look so young,
pressed into the blurred town.
All that's left is the rattling,

a memory of salt,
my hand pressed against the glass
sifting your hair from rain.

At the End

tongue closed and blue
as autumn crocus

it is night
and you are close
but all the seeds we scattered
have been pecked away

we lie
like smashed shells
    on the rock
where thrushes
suck out snail meat

a bitter scrape of moon
at the window –
        all is quiet
in this cautious undergrowth

                blood burns like fire
                without a vent

Tears Like Lava

Two little people
stand fossilised,
their love frozen
their bodies stone
joined in deathly matrimony,
Siamese by destruction.

They smile at winter,
stare at the sun.
The weather
wears them down.
They stand
crying;
tears like lava.

The Reflection Answers Narcissus

I held on (couldn't help myself)
to the idea, just the idea,
         of love.

I gripped like a monkey
to the bottom, just the bottom,
         of a tree.

And all I could see amongst the high, echoing leaves
was your face (like a star dribbling into stars)
         mouthing one word:

         Enough

Off the Map

I have fallen off the map.
Walked into the white spaces
beyond Purgatory, homeward
under blue to the bird-sodden
        solitudes of silence.

Here, time folds and refolds itself
under dying ash. A woodpecker
drunk on the echo of its beat
marks out a flurry of confusion
        in impenetrable code.

Do not follow me. Not yet.
This little world is barren
but for the birds' skewed music,
the wild garlic's wasting stench.
        No map is perfect

until it is seeded with symbols,
hills, the slow tangle of direction.
In this white silence, they grow
stealthy as longing
        for the sound of your voice.

Holiday in Arden

i

Easy in Arden's woods to fall in love
almost without knowing that you have.

All things are triggers:
words sharp as yew daggers;

cupping psalms of light on leaf; the arch
of peace beneath a parasol of beech.

Laughter shimmers like summer rain
in this maze of trees, this tangled shrine.

Billows into passion like puffballs
from the rot of sorrows left to fall.

ii

Off goes Ganymede after boys intent on stealing sticks,
loping like a deer into the wood. Orlando watches him,
his pen ignored for once, still unclear why Ganymede insists

on playing games. *Just call me Rosalind, or better, Ros,*
Ganymede insists, and so he does, creates
a whole new language of unresisting love

without ever knowing he's addressing Rosalind
for real. So strange after a fortnight of this idyll
when all's revealed, the masks come off, and Rosalind's

ablaze in all her glory, like the first clear sun of spring.
But here's the thing. This Rosalind's been hitched already
to some other Duke.   Honour interferes.

iii

Orlando meets a girl from Arden
on the streetside back at home.

They settle down, try for children.
He gives Rosalind to the foam

of dream and forced forgetting.
Time's gentle dragging of the comb.

iv

...but Rosalind keeps on appearing at parties,
drunk and flirtatious. Orlando breathes her in,
moves on in fretful honour, his courage
lost in wine and longing.

The forest seems far and yet too close,
a haunting of trees. The girl from Arden
becomes untouchable with anything but words.
Orlando starts another poem:

> *Easy in Arden's woods to fall in love*
> *almost without knowing that you have...*

Love Poem Disguised as a Fairy Tale
after Madame D'Aulnoy

In her eyes, the girl she was; the hard
unthinking rifle-shot of youth. They are urgent
as a cat's yowl in the dark rooms of home
where nothing matters but the way a fish
lifts wet, unspeaking from the plate.

She is deer now, but for those eyes.
They dance through me, demanding to be spared.
Another life is on her.

She whispers from the soft
purse of her deer's mouth that she still has much to do.
I love her and I always have. I never saw her until now.
I will return to my palace of books
hungry though I cannot eat for thinking of her

as she runs through the bright wood, a spare
change of terror jangling in her girl's eyes,
crab apples crunching like years beneath her feet.

My hunt is over. All I can do is wait
for the changes to cease, for the drifting powers
that drive her to other skins to calm
their churning, for her to find me again
with her girl's eyes and hope

that the woman she's becoming under feather,
hide and scale can see beyond the way
I've learned in her absence to stiffen, like a startled deer.

Last Thoughts of the Unicorn
after T.H. White

Blood in the forest, its scent a hammer beat
under the drum of rain. Blood.

In the forest, high voices.
Almost-children carrying blood
loose under their skins as they pulse
through artery tunnels of trees.

The trees, which seep
soporific languages of blood,
guide them through labyrinths
         to the taut centre.

Blood in the forest scent. The drum
a hammer in the beaten rain. Blood.

She collapses by a tree. I watch
as she moves like one grown
to the full capacity of blood.
Boys come with rituals

to bind her laughter to the oak.
The forest stills to a hiss.
A scrape of metal. Sun
cutting godfaces in the leaves.

The blood drum. A forest hammer.
Rain to the beat of scent. Blood.

An itch in the shadows, blood rising
in the dark at my approach.
She trembles. Specks tears. Guides
my horn to her lap. Ecstatic. Slow.

Blood in the forest. The hammer
slowed to the synthesis of blood.
Song of metal in the undergrowth.
                              Blood.

Fragment of a Fairy Tale Caught in a Time Loop

he came struggling
through the thorns
his sword out and his horse
struggling through the thorns he came
breathing damp through the dense
forest he came struggling
through his sword through his horse
through the forest he came
breathing damp
a taste of love like rose petals
struggling through the thorns
his horse like rose petals
through the forest
his sword breathing damp
in the dense forest a taste
of love and his horse
struggling through
the thorns his sword his horse
breathing damp like rose petals
in the dense forest
struggling struggling
whispering your name

Thisbë the Verse

HIM
The past is a rattle of change on the desk
counted afterhours in a dark shop
where plants leer like the tongues of wolves
and the last lick of daylight tugs
at the letterbox, calling tomorrow to account.

HER
Come with me! I have been learning
how to turn money into light. Just
take two coins and post them to my tongue.
I will drown the howl of their histories
in my saliva and pass them back, transformed.

HIM
The phone roars like a hungry lion,
drowns out reason. Was that a voice
through the letterbox? I am too tired for words.
My mouth is dry and all the graves I've ever known
are gaping at me in imitation of a kiss.

Some Kind of Fairy Tale

What have you brought
from the top of the keep?

A heart in my mouth.
A lover's leap.

What did you learn
from the bones of the past?

The horror of finding
my heart in a cast.

What did you gain
from love's first stroke?

A river's roar.
A raven's croak.

Why have you hidden it
for all these years?

I was afraid to reach
through the river of tears.

And why are you stood here
answering still?

It takes time for resolve
to equal skill.

Beyond the Gates

What we took from the garden
was love, for love is knowledge
and the knowledge of love
is a bitter seed in the belly of a bird.
         Expelled over new lands
the seed falls as love into the soil,
casts out slender roots to grow
and seed and grow again,
carried further and further
         from the garden
in unending chains of fruiting trees.
The trees hold the garden as memory
in a lover's embrace, as the sun
is sucked by leaves, consumed
         in adoration and exchange.
And age becomes knowledge
becomes love as their trunks swell
over time into rings, and each ring
binds us to the garden because
         what we took from the garden
was love, and love was the garden
and it is the garden that keeps us
breathing each other in
here in the cold land beyond its gates
         as it pumps through our hearts
                  like blood.

Love Like Pollen

Love like pollen
first a fine dust of it
smearing the summer air
then, sticky and heavy
on the backs of bees
the high priests of flower marriages
travelling from bloom to gaping bloom

Love like pollen
pistil and chamber gorged, expectant
stems trembling
unsteady with want
craving the caress
of fine wings and endless legs
at the wedding's end

The Marriage of Consonant and Vowel

i *After the Wedding*

Dreamt of you again last night,
your smiling face pushed close to mine;
caught between mirrors, a squeezebox
of repeats cluttering the line.

I thought as we were twitter-pressed
like sausage meat inside new skins
how little's known of what we love
or hate and how compression bins

our excess dreams and sears off
the vowels of love; the consonants
of hurt are all that's left intact.
How does a lover thrive? Expanse!

Not questing after jagged and reductive fact
but after puffball spores and seedlings of romance.

ii *The Bride Has Taken the Vwls & Lft th Bldng*

Drmt f y gn lst nt
yr :) pshd cls 2 mn;
cght btwn mrrrs, sqzbx
f rpts clttrng th ln.

Thght s w wr twttr-prssd
lke ssg mt nsd nw skns
hw lttl's knwn f wht w ♥
r h8 & hw cmprssn bns

r xs drms & srs ff
th vwls f ♥; th cnsnnts
f hrt r ll tht's lft ntct.
Hw ds lvr thrv? Xpns!

Nt qstng ftr jggd & rdctv fct
bt ftr pffbll sprs & sdlngs f rmnc.

iii *The Bride in Her Lover's Bed*

ea o ou aai a i,
ou ii ae ue oe o ie;
au eee io a ueeeo
o eea uei e ie.

i ou a e ee ie-ee
ie auae ea iie e i
o ie o o a e oe
o ae a o oeio i

ou ee ea a ea o
e oe o oe; e ooa
o u ae a a e ia.
o oe a oe ie? Eae!

o uei ae ae a euie a
u ae ua oe a eei o oae.

Coda

The documents of foiled need
are a lined face, corrupted flesh;
the papers onto which you bleed
until the book's a bloody mesh

      which even lovers can't translate
      for fear of opening old scars.
      It takes a tongue to find a mate
      who'll recognise your song; the stars

by which you navigate a dream
of touch and understanding. Hope.
A mouth you train to rarely scream,
far-focused as a telescope.

      A light, not born of want and blood,
      still visible when all else fails,
      which floats above the rising flood
      of love, and other fairy tales.

Indigo Dreams Publishing Ltd
24, Forest Houses
Cookworthy Moor
Halwill
Beaworthy
Devon
EX21 5UU
www.indigodreams.co.uk